WILDLIFE WORLDS

EUROPE

Tim Harris

W
FRANKLIN WATTS
LONDON · SYDNEY

Franklin Watts

First published in Great Britain in 2019 by The Watts Publishing Group

Copyright © The Watts Publishing Group, 2019

HB ISBN: 978 1 4451 6727 5

PB ISBN: 978 1 4451 6728 2

Printed in Dubai

Series Editor: Amy Pimperton

Series Designer: Nic Davies smartdesignstudio.co.uk

Picture researchers: Rachelle Morris (Nature Picture Library),
Laura Sutherland (Nature Picture Library), Diana Morris

Picture credits:

Alamy: Amanda Pharyos 15tl.
Nature PL: Ingo Amdt 15tr; Barry Bland 29br; Juan Manuel Borrero 22br; Peter Cairns 2b, 28c; Stephen Dalton 9br, 19b; Martin Gabriel 3c, 17bc; Angelo Gandolfi 22–23t; Patricio Robles Gil front cover b; Erland Haarland 21t; Klein & Hubert 17bl; Pete Oxford 21bl; Michel Poinsignan 7tr; Jean E Roche 18–19c; The Big Picture 24; Nick Upton 12bl; Markus Varesvuo: 17c; Wild Wonders of Europe/Orsolya Haarberg 27br/Giesbers 17br/Lilja 6b/ Lundgren 9bl/ Smit 8–9t/Varesvuo 15b/Zupanc 16; Sven Zacek 11tr.
Shutterstock: Belizar 3t, 8bl; Biggunsband 12–13c; Bildagenteur Zoonar GmbH 3b, 19tr; Aleksander Bolbot back cover tl, 2t, 10–11c; Mike Caunt front cover t, 25tc; Chuckstop 5c; Daniel Dunca back cover tr, 23br; Frank Fichtmueller 23tr; Giedrilus 4b, 25c, 32t; Paulis Giovanni 7tl; liluta goean 9cr; Andrey Gudkov 19tl, 30t; J. Helgason 26–27c, 31t; Jaro68 17tl; Lukas Juocas 29cl; Szczepan Klejbuk 1, 11b; Piotr Krzeslak 21br; Liane M 20c, 20bl; Pablo Manzi 5t; Mark Medcalf 4t; Marek Mierzejewski 25tl; Ondrej Prosicky 27bl; Ben Queenborough 25tr; Stella Photography back cover tcr, 14bl, 30b; Andrew Sutton 29t; Marek R Swadzba back cover tcl, 5b, 10bl, 13cr; Taviphoto 13b; Wead 14t; k west 6–7c; Shaun Wilkinson 13tr; Vladimir Wrangel 26bl, 32b.

Every attempt has been made to
clear copyright. Should there be any
inadvertent omission please apply
to the publisher for rectification.

Franklin Watts

An imprint of

Hachette Children's Group

Part of The Watts Publishing Group

Carmelite House

50 Victoria Embankment

London EC4Y 0DZ

An Hachette UK Company

www.hachette.co.uk

www.franklinwatts.co.uk

With thanks to the Nature Picture Library

Contents

European Continent

The European continent is surrounded by the Arctic and Atlantic Oceans to the north and west, and the Mediterranean Sea and the Black Sea to the south. In the east, it is separated from Asia by the Ural and Caucasus Mountains.

Europe's climate varies enormously. In the far north, temperatures remain below freezing throughout the winter months. The great plains of Russia and Eastern Europe are freezing in winter, but baking hot in summer. Southern Europe has a pleasant Mediterranean climate: hot and dry in summer and warm for the rest of the year. About one-third of Europe is covered by forest. There are also large areas of natural grassland, but no deserts or rainforest.

ATLANTIC PUFFIN

Europe has several high mountain ranges, including the Alps and the Pyrenees.

RED DEER

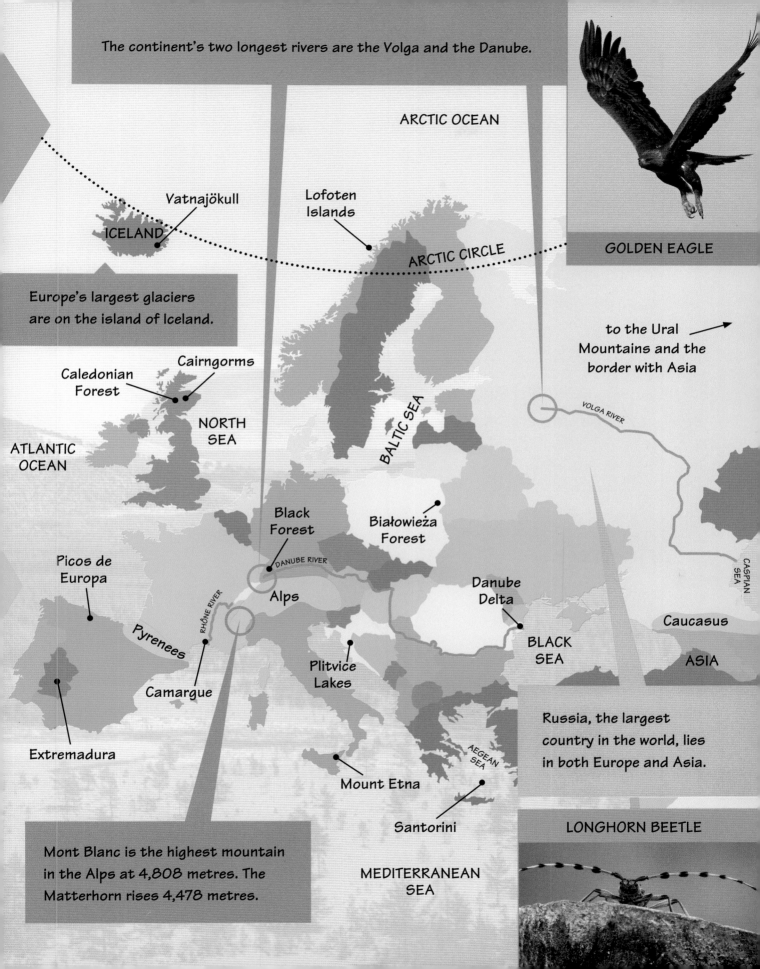

The continent's two longest rivers are the Volga and the Danube.

ARCTIC OCEAN

Vatnajökull

Lofoten
Islands

ICELAND

ARCTIC CIRCLE

GOLDEN EAGLE

Europe's largest glaciers
are on the island of Iceland.

to the Ural
Mountains and the
border with Asia

Caledonian
Forest

Cairngorms

VOLGA RIVER

NORTH
SEA

BALTIC SEA

ATLANTIC
OCEAN

Black
Forest

Białowieża
Forest

CASPIAN
SEA

Picos de
Europa

DANUBE RIVER

Danube
Delta

Caucasus

Pyrenees

RHÔNE RIVER

Alps

BLACK
SEA

ASIA

Camargue

Plitvice
Lakes

Extremadura

Russia, the largest
country in the world, lies
in both Europe and Asia.

AEGEAN
SEA

Mount Etna

Santorini

LONGHORN BEETLE

Mont Blanc is the highest mountain
in the Alps at 4,808 metres. The
Matterhorn rises 4,478 metres.

MEDITERRANEAN
SEA

Santorini

In the Aegean Sea, south-east of mainland Greece, the islands of Santorini (Thira), Therasia and Aspronisi surround a large, oval lagoon that measures about 12 kilometres from one side to the other.

The islands are all that remain of an ancient volcano that erupted violently about 3,600 years ago. Gigantic cliffs of volcanic rock rise out of the ocean. Villages of white-washed houses are built into the steep slopes. The islands have no rivers and no lakes because rain soaks straight into the porous rocks.

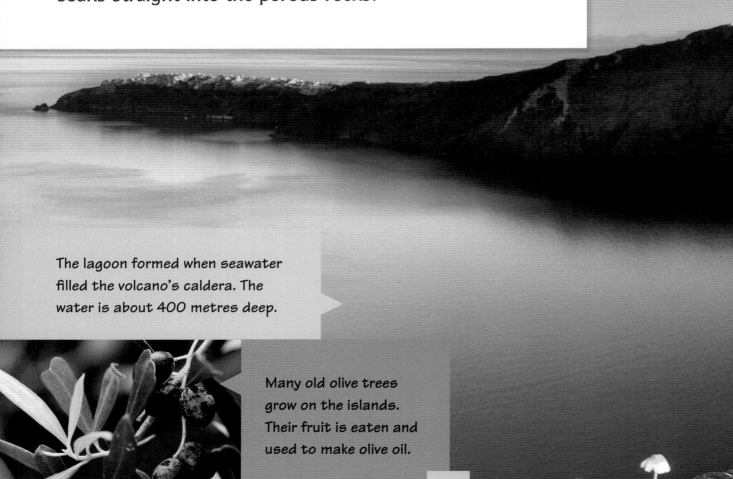

The lagoon formed when seawater filled the volcano's caldera. The water is about 400 metres deep.

Many old olive trees grow on the islands. Their fruit is eaten and used to make olive oil.

Eleonora's falcons build their nests on cliffs, from where they fly quickly in pursuit of dragonflies and small birds.

Praying mantids, like this European mantis, are large insects that grab prey with their front legs.

7

Danube River

The source of Europe's second-longest river is in Germany's Black Forest. The Danube grows ever-wider as it meanders 2,850 kilometres through ten countries on its way to the Black Sea. Many of Europe's great cities are built beside the river.

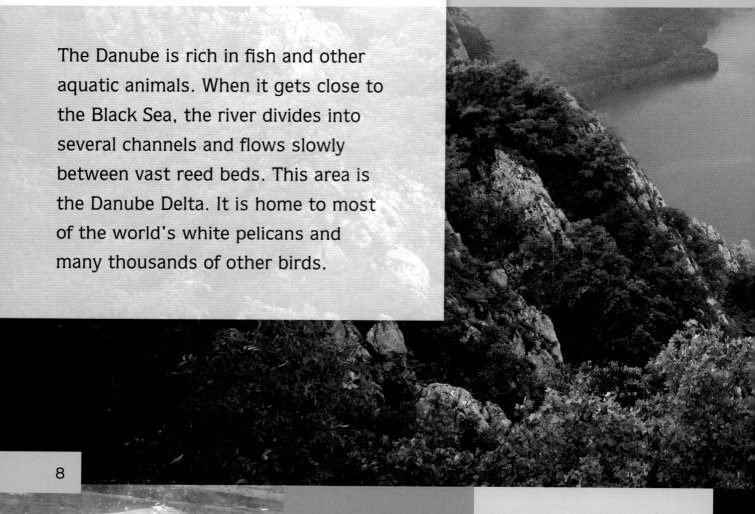

The Danube is rich in fish and other aquatic animals. When it gets close to the Black Sea, the river divides into several channels and flows slowly between vast reed beds. This area is the Danube Delta. It is home to most of the world's white pelicans and many thousands of other birds.

8

Sleek otters are playful animals that swim fast underwater to catch fish.

The Danube sturgeon is now a very rare fish. It can grow more than 2 metres long and swims from the Black Sea up the river to lay its eggs.

The Danube flows through forests, farmland and marshes on its way to the Black Sea.

GREAT WHITE PELICAN

A male emperor dragonfly will defend its territory from other dragonflies.

Białowieża Forest

A huge, ancient forest once covered most of Eastern Europe. Although most of it has been cut down for farmland, one large area survives: Białowieża Forest.

Białowieża is a dense forest of spruce, pine, alder, oak and birch trees. Many are very old. One tree, the Patriarch Oak, is more than 550 years old. All of the world's wild European bison live in the forest, which is also home to woodpeckers, storks and birds of prey. Many beautiful flowers grow in its wet meadows.

Many butterflies fly in and around the forest, including the stunning Camberwell beauty.

The forest is dense. When trees fall, they create openings in the canopy, which allow sunshine to reach the forest floor. This encourages young trees to grow. Dead trees provide nest holes for woodpeckers and homes for insects and many other invertebrates.

Black woodpeckers drill holes in trees with their beaks to feed on invertebrates living inside.

The European bison is Europe's largest endemic land animal.

Plitvice Lakes

In the Velebit Mountains of Croatia, the Korana River tumbles down rapids and waterfalls. It passes through 16 lakes, each one of which is lower than the previous one. This is one of the most beautiful places in Europe.

Surrounding the crystal-clear waters of the lakes are woods and meadows. Trout and other fish swim in the lakes. Bears, wolves, wildcats and lynx live in the forest. Colourful orchids and other wildflowers grow in the meadows and bats make their homes in the many caves in the limestone rocks.

Veliki Slap is the highest of the waterfalls at Plitvice. Water falls 78 metres over a limestone cliff to splash into the lake below.

Lynx are fearsome predators. As well as hunting on the ground, they can climb trees and they even swim to catch fish.

Many different kinds of insects live at Plitvice, including dragonflies, butterflies and blue-and-black longhorn beetles (below).

The most venomous snake in Croatia is the horned viper.

Mount Etna

Mount Etna, on the Italian island of Sicily, is one of the biggest and most active volcanoes in the world. Every few years, spectacular explosive eruptions burst from one of the four craters at its summit.

Few animals live around the top of the volcano, but the vineyards, chestnut groves and apple orchards on its lower slopes support porcupines, foxes and wildcats. Eagles, buzzards and falcons hunt small mammals and birds.

Local people roast chestnuts from sweet chestnut trees, some of which are hundreds of years old.

In December 2015, Mount Etna erupted at night, lighting up the sky. A plume (cloud) of ash was sent 3 kilometres into the atmosphere.

If threatened, a crested porcupine charges back-end first into its attacker to stab it with its sharp quills (spines).

The Mediterranean black widow spider can give a very painful bite if annoyed.

Bee-eaters' favourite foods are bees and wasps. Before eating their prey, these multicoloured birds bash the bee or wasp on a hard surface to kill it and to remove the sting.

Alps

The Alps form Europe's highest mountain range. Hundreds of peaks rise more than 3,000 metres above sea level. Glaciers have carved them into jagged shapes, with knife-like ridges and pointed summits.

16

Broadleaved trees, such as oak, beech and ash, grow on the lower slopes and are replaced by pine trees and dwarf shrubs at greater altitudes. Above the tree line, alpine meadows are covered with snow for most of the year, but are awash with colourful flowers in summer. Ibex (mountain goats), marmots and bears are some of the animals that live in the mountains.

The Matterhorn is one of the highest mountains in the Alps, towering dramatically over the landscape. Its sides are so steep that no one managed to climb to its summit until 1865.

A golden eagle is strong enough to pick a marmot or rabbit from the ground in its talons, then kill the prey with its hooked beak.

Alpine marmots hibernate in burrows during the winter months.

Fire salamanders live in the foothills of the Alps. They spend much of their time hidden under logs or rocks.

The small yellow-and-white flowers of edelweiss bloom when the mountain snow melts between July and September.

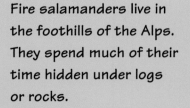

Camargue

Where the mighty Rhône River meets the Mediterranean Sea on the south coast of France lies Europe's largest delta. This vast marshy plain has many lakes and pools surrounded by reed beds.

Flamingos, herons and other long-legged birds wade in the shallow waters in search of food. Eagles, harriers and other birds of prey hunt overhead, and thousands of warblers and other small birds build their nests in the reeds. Camargue horses and cattle graze on the grasslands between the lakes.

Many of the Camargue's large reed beds are where thousands of small birds, mammals and amphibians make their homes.

Herds of Camargue horses run wild through the marshes.

Penduline tits build a nest that hangs from the twig of a tree. The nest is made from animal hair, spiders' webs and bits of leaf.

Male Mediterranean tree frogs call 'cra-a-ar' in spring to attract mates. The noise of the springtime frog chorus can be deafening!

Extremadura

In winter, the rolling grasslands of this region of Spain are wet and bleak, but in spring they warm up and come alive with the blooms of millions of wildflowers. In midsummer, the region becomes baking hot and dry.

While some areas are treeless, other places have open woodland called *dehesa* (woodland and grass), where thousands of long-necked, long-legged birds called cranes feed on fallen acorns during the winter. In spring, these birds fly away to breeding grounds, but they are replaced by colourful bee-eaters and rollers that have migrated from Africa.

Cattle graze among the trees of the *dehesa* landscape.

Rollers often perch prominently on posts, trees or overhead wires. From here they watch for small snakes, mice or frogs, which they swoop down on to eat.

The venom of the beautifully patterned false smooth snake will kill a lizard, but is harmless to humans.

Many cranes spend the winter in Extremadura, but they breed much farther north in Scandinavia (Denmark, Norway and Sweden).

Picos de Europa

A range of mountains rises dramatically near the northern coast of Spain. Called the Picos de Europa, this range has been shaped by slow-moving glaciers and the action of running water.

NARANJO DE BULNES

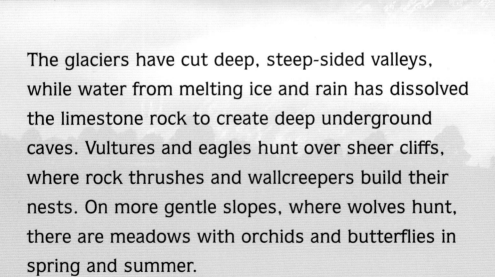

The glaciers have cut deep, steep-sided valleys, while water from melting ice and rain has dissolved the limestone rock to create deep underground caves. Vultures and eagles hunt over sheer cliffs, where rock thrushes and wallcreepers build their nests. On more gentle slopes, where wolves hunt, there are meadows with orchids and butterflies in spring and summer.

The bright yellow flowers of Pyrenean lilies can be seen from May to July, but only at high altitudes.

Since they are almost vertical, the sides of Naranjo de Bulnes are a challenge for any rock-climber. The summit of the mountain is more than 2,500 metres high.

Sure-footed chamois are ideally adapted to climb the very steep slopes.

More than 150 different kinds of butterfly live in the Picos de Europa, including the spectacular swallowtail.

Colourful wallcreepers are at home on bare rock faces.

Caledonian Forest

Pine forest has grown in the highlands of Scotland for about 9,000 years. Although much of the forest has been cut down, some large areas remain.

The forest is home to red deer, pine martens, red squirrels and a few wildcats. Ospreys plunge feet-first into the slow-moving waters of the Spey River to catch salmon and other fish. Crossbills feed on pine cones, while large birds called capercaillies eat evergreen needle-shaped leaves during the winter, when snow carpets the ground.

Pine forest cloaks the lower slopes of the Cairngorm Mountains. The tops of the mountains are treeless and are often buried in cloud. Freshwater lakes – called lochs – within the forest are home to swans, ducks and other water birds.

Atlantic salmon swim from the ocean to spawn upstream in rivers, such as the Spey.

Named for their colour, strawberry spiders live in damp clearings in the forest.

Crested tits live their whole lives in the forest.

Each autumn, rival male red deer fight each other for dominance. These battles, called ruts, can be very violent.

25

Iceland

In the far north of the Atlantic Ocean, the island of Iceland sits just below the Arctic Circle. Icy glaciers, including Europe's largest, Vatnajökull, cover much of its surface. It also has many active and dormant volcanoes.

Rivers carrying meltwater from glaciers plunge over spectacular waterfalls on their way to the ocean. There are hundreds of geysers – fountains of boiling water that regularly spurt from the ground. Although the island is cold and windy for much of the year, it is mild enough in the summer to support many birds and flowering plants. There are no native reptiles or amphibians.

Edible sea urchins live on the seabed in coastal waters around Iceland. They feed on barnacles and marine worms.

The Arctic fox, which has snow-white fur in winter, is Iceland's only native land mammal.

Ice caves form during the summer when water carves out 'canals' beneath a glacier, such as Vatnajökull. In winter, it is too cold for water to flow, so the 'canal' becomes an empty cave.

From March onwards, harlequin ducks return to fast-flowing rivers to raise their young. They spend the winter at the coast.

Lofoten Islands

Situated off the coast of northern Norway, this group of islands rises spectacularly from the ocean. Sheer cliffs rise from the sea, with thousands of seabirds nesting on their ledges. Narrow inlets, such as Trollfjord, were carved by ancient glaciers.

The snow-dusted cliffs of Festhelltinden Mountain loom over red fishermen's cabins.

There are six major islands and hundreds of smaller ones. Despite being north of the Arctic Circle, temperatures rise above freezing even during the winter because of the warming effect of the Norwegian Sea. Millions of fish breed around the islands, and the world's largest deepwater coral reef lies offshore – as well as some of the world's deadliest currents.

Whales, including sperm whales, visit the waters around the islands.

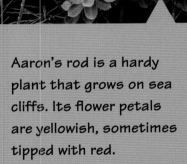

Aaron's rod is a hardy plant that grows on sea cliffs. Its flower petals are yellowish, sometimes tipped with red.

Thousands of Atlantic puffins dive underwater to catch sand eels with their amazing beaks. They dig burrows in which to nest.

Glossary

altitude the height of an object above sea level

aquatic living in water

caldera large volcanic crater, usually formed by a major eruption, after which the crater collapses

canopy the highest tree branches in a forest

coral reef a hard structure in the sea that is made from the remains of dead coral

current water that is moving in one direction

delta the area where a river drops its sediment as it enters a lake or the ocean

dense where trees and shrubs grow close together

desert a place that receives little or no rainfall and has few plants or none at all

dormant inactive for now

endemic a plant or animal native to a particular place

eruptions explosive blasts from volcanoes

glacier a large body of ice moving slowly down a valley

hardy able to cope with harsh conditions, such as extreme cold or heat

hibernate a very long, deep sleep, usually in winter

inlet a narrow sea channel that runs inland

invertebrate animal that doesn't have a backbone

lagoon an area of salt water enclosed by a coral reef, sandbank or rocks

limestone sedimentary rock made of fossilised animal skeletons and shells

marine living in the ocean

meander to wind first one way, then the other

meltwater water that results from glacier ice melting, usually in summer

migrated travelled a long way to take advantage of more plentiful food

porous having many small holes that soak up water

predator animal that hunts and eats other animals

prey animals that are eaten by other animals

reed beds large areas of reeds

saline salt water

source the place where a river starts

spawning when a fish or amphibian releases or deposits its eggs

summit the very top

territories areas that some animals defend during the breeding season

venom chemicals that some animals, such as snakes, use to kill or injure prey

venomous producing chemicals that can injure or kill prey

vineyard where grapes are grown, usually to make wine

Books

Animal Families (series) by Tim Harris (Wayland, 2014)
Close-up Continents: Mapping Europe by Paul Rockett (Franklin Watts, 2016)
Europe: Endangered Animals by Grace Jones (Booklife, 2018)
Infomojis: Continents by Jon Richards and Ed Simkins (Wayland, 2019)

Websites

Europe Facts for Kids
Lots of interesting and fun facts on the European continent.
www.kids-world-travel-guide.com/europe-facts.html

Geography for Kids
Has profiles of every country in Europe.
www.ducksters.com/geography/europe.php

Go Wild
Discover more about your favourite animals in these WWF fact files.
gowild.wwf.org.uk/regions/europe-fact-files

National Geographic Animal Pictures and Facts
Simply type in the animals you're interested in and get lots of fascinating facts. Covers mammals, reptiles, amphibians, fish and birds.
www.nationalgeographic.com/animals/index/

Further information

Index